MICHELANGELO

MICHEL

Published by Oxford University Press

NGELO

A Biography by
ELIZABETH RIPLEY

With Drawings,
Paintings and Sculpture by
Michelangelo

HENRY Z. WALCK, INCORPORATED, DISTRIBUTORS · NEW YORK 1953

ILLUSTRATIONS

MICHELANGELO

One spring morning in 1475 a son was born to Ludovico Buonarotti, governor of a village in Italy. The boy was named Michelangelo. His mother died when he was very little, so his father sent him to live in the home of a stonecutter.

This man and his wife cared for the little Michelangelo as if he were their son. When he was old enough to play alone he loved to run wild through the stone quarries and watch men cutting blocks of marble from the side of the hill. One day he found some charcoal and began to draw pictures on pieces of smooth marble. He would carve the pictures into statues, he thought.

Michelangelo lived with the stonecutter's family until he was ten. Then his father, who lived in the city of Florence, sent for him. It was time for him to go to school. He would live with his father and four brothers and study Latin every day.

Michelangelo hated school. He told his father that he wanted to draw pictures and become a great artist. His father replied severely that gentlemen did not become painters, and his brothers laughed at him and told him that he would never make any money. But the boy continued to draw.

One day Ludovico heard that a well known painter had praised his son's drawings. Perhaps the boy should learn painting, he decided, and he arranged to send him to the school of a famous painter named Ghirlandaio.

Michelangelo was thirteen when he went to live in the home of his teacher. He was happy now because he could draw all the time. Often Ghirlandaio asked his pupil to help him on the pictures he was painting. Confidently Michelangelo sketched in figures, which looked so lifelike that the master wondered if the quick tempered boy who sometimes answered him so rudely knew more about drawing than he did.

It was not only in Ghirlandaio's studio that Michelangelo learned to draw. He used to spend hours studying the works of other artists. In the Church of Santa Croce he admired the paintings of the great Giotto, who had lived two hundred years before, and he tried to capture this strong, simple style in the copies he made of Giotto's noble figures.

**DRAWING FROM GIOTTO'S FRESCOES
IN SANTA CROCE, FLORENCE**

Louvre, Paris

For two years Michelangelo helped Ghirlandaio paint pictures. One day he corrected the outline of one of his teacher's figures, and suddenly it came to life. It stood out from the background as if it had been carved. The boy was really a sculptor, Ghirlandaio thought, and he decided to talk the matter over with Ludovico.

Reluctantly Ludovico consented to send his son to a school for sculptors which had been founded by the brilliant and ambitious ruler of Florence, Lorenzo de' Medici. Without regret Michelangelo said good-bye to his teacher and began to learn the art of sculpture. He loved to feel the mallet and chisel in his hand. The sound of hammering on stone rang in his ears from morning to night, and he was happy. Sometimes he took his work to a nearby garden which Lorenzo de' Medici had filled with beautiful Greek and Roman sculpture. He spent hours studying the antique statues, and copied many of them.

One day he was cutting away bits of marble from an antique mask which he was making when he heard a strange voice behind him. Turning around, he saw a richly dressed man with an ugly face and keen eyes who was examining his work intently. The man was Lorenzo de' Medici, who was called the Magnificent. The boy explained that he was making a mask of an antique faun. If the faun was old, Lorenzo said, it should lack some teeth. Then he walked away. When he returned the next day some of the teeth were missing. Lorenzo made no comment, but asked the boy to send his father to see him.

Ludovico Buonarotti put on his best clothes and hurried to the palace. Lorenzo received him cordially and told him that he believed Michelangelo could become a brilliant sculptor who would bring fame to Florence. He asked that the boy be allowed to live in his palace. He offered Ludovico any reward for giving up his son. The modest father asked for a job in the customs office, which Lorenzo gladly granted him. Elated, Ludovico hurried home to tell the good news to Michelangelo.

COPY OF ANTIQUE FAUN
National Museum, Florence

Photo Anderson

Dressed in the fine new suit Lorenzo had given him, Michelangelo walked through the halls of the Medici Palace. All around him were priceless treasures. He saw beautiful vases from Greece, shining coins from many countries, and glowing oil paintings by the greatest artists of Italy. He admired the simple beauty of the marble statues from ancient Greece. The sculptors who had lived many years before could teach him a great deal, he thought.

In the evening he sat at a long table in the Medici dining room and listened to the brilliant conversation of Lorenzo and his guests. All the best known philosophers, poets, and artists were entertained at Lorenzo's table. They discussed Greek philosophy and quoted Latin verse. Often the fifteen-year-old Michelangelo was asked to sit next to Lorenzo while well known artists sat at the far end of the table.

Sometimes he sat next to the tutor of the Medici children, who told him fascinating stories from the old Greek myths. He loved especially the story of the battle of the centaurs. These strange creatures, half man, half horse, had been invited to the wedding of a Greek king. In the middle of the ceremony they seized the bride and tried to carry her away. A furious battle followed. Michelangelo could picture the scene vividly. He sketched it on a block of flat marble. Then he chipped away pieces from the stone so that the figures stood out from the background. This was called a bas-relief.

The Battle of the Centaurs was a violent tangle of figures. Michelangelo was so pleased that he had been able to carve the furious scene which he had pictured vividly in his mind that he never gave the bas-relief away.

BATTLE OF CENTAURS
Buonarotti Museum, Florence

The days in Lorenzo's palace were happy ones for Michelangelo, and his happiest moments were when he was working with mallet and chisel. As bits of stone fell away from the block of marble, he could see his thoughts emerge from the stone. This was his greatest joy.

He did not know how to take part in the gay life of the other students. Because he knew he was ugly, he felt shy and often sad. He feared that the boys his own age were making fun of him, and this made him angry and rude. His fellow students admired his work, but they found it hard to like him.

One boy especially resented his ugly manner, and because he was not a good sculptor himself he was jealous of Michelangelo. His name was Torrigiano. One day while the students were at work Michelangelo answered Torrigiano's taunts with an angry insult. With one swift, powerful blow Torrigiano knocked Michelangelo to the floor. When the other boys rushed to revive him they found that his nose was badly broken. Torrigiano had made him uglier than before, and the melancholy boy became even sadder for he knew that he would have to go through life with a flattened and misshapen nose.

PORTRAIT OF MICHELANGELO
ATTRIBUTED TO MARCELLO VENUSTI
Capitol Museum, Rome

Photo Anderson

There was a hospital in the monastery of San Spirito where the monks cared for the poor people of Florence. Michelangelo used to visit the hospital often, for the monks had given him permission to examine the bodies of the people who had died.

By the flickering light of a candle he dissected many corpses. He noted how the muscles were connected and how the joints moved. Then he drew pictures of what he saw. The foulness of the decaying corpses sickened him, but he never stopped his absorbing work. The more he learned about the construction of the human form, the more Michelangelo marvelled at its great beauty, and he made many wonderful drawings of the human figure.

STUDY OF NUDE TORSO
AND VARIOUS HEADS
Ashmolean Museum, Oxford

Some people in Florence thought it was wrong to dissect corpses. The study of anatomy was wicked, they said, and Michelangelo was a sinner. But the artist who found such beauty in the human form was also deeply religious.

Often he went to the church of San Marco to listen to the fiery sermons of a fierce, black-hooded monk named Savonarola. The monk had a huge hooked nose and sallow skin, but his eyes glowed like coals as he hurled words of warning at the people of Florence. Unmerciful destruction would come to the city, he thundered, unless Lorenzo and his people gave up the worship of the pagan art of Greece and Rome and went back to the teachings of Jesus. Michelangelo was greatly moved. Although he was inspired by the beauty of pagan art, he had a deep faith in God. At the same time that he was carving the Battle of the Centaurs he was working on a bas-relief of a beautiful Madonna and Child.

The monumental figure of the Madonna sits at the foot of a flight of stairs. Perhaps Michelangelo was thinking of his own mother and the stairs outside the cottage where he was born. When people saw Michelangelo's Madonna, they were amazed and perplexed. The beautifully draped figure has the physical vigor of a pagan statue, but it expresses at the same time the purity of spirit of the Mother of Christ. Michelangelo had created something startlingly new.

MADONNA OF THE STAIRS
Buonarotti Museum, Florence

Michelangelo lived in the Medici Palace for two years. Lorenzo gave him fine clothes, pocket money, and a room of his own. Then one spring day Lorenzo died, and his blundering son Piero became the ruler of Florence. Piero paid no attention to the young sculptor; so Michelangelo packed his tools in a bundle and went back to his father's home.

The glorious age of Lorenzo, who had been called the Magnificent, was over. The powerful army of the king of France swept down on Italy and the foolish Piero did nothing to defend his city. Michelangelo was terror stricken.

Early one crisp October morning he put his money in a purse, mounted a horse, and rode in the direction of Venice. Two young artists rode with him, for he had offered to pay their expenses. But Michelangelo's money didn't last long. After a few days the three youths were riding back to Florence. At the gates of Bologna they were stopped by the police because they had not paid the city tax. The young men were standing with long faces, not knowing what to do, when a richly dressed gentleman approached them. His name was Aldovrandi, he told them. He loved sculpture and had admired Michelangelo's Battle of the Centaurs. He invited the sculptor to visit him and offered to pay the tax for the young men. Michelangelo was delighted. He handed what was left of his purse to his companions and wished them a safe return to Florence. Then he rode home with Aldovrandi.

He lived with the wealthy nobleman for over a year. The days passed pleasantly. Aldovrandi loved poetry and asked his companion to read to him until he fell asleep. He arranged to have Michelangelo carve two statues for the tomb of Saint Dominic in Bologna. One of them was a beautiful kneeling angel holding a candlestick. Aldovrandi was delighted and Michelangelo was paid well for the job, but the artists in Bologna were jealous and threatened to get rid of the Florentine sculptor. Michelangelo feared for his life when he walked through the dark streets at night. He missed his family, too, and so one day he sewed his money in his doublet and set out across the hills toward Florence.

KNEELING ANGEL
WITH A CANDLESTICK
Saint Dominic's, Bologna

Michelangelo was glad to be home again. His brothers didn't laugh at him now, for he had brought money from Bologna. He hired a studio, bought a block of marble, and started to carve a statue of a sleeping Cupid.

One cold January morning a messenger from the Medici Palace knocked at his door. Piero de' Medici wanted to see him at once. Michelangelo wrapped himself in a cloak and plowed through the snow to the palace. Piero greeted him enthusiastically. He told him that he planned to give a party that evening and he wanted the sculptor to build a huge snow man in the courtyard. Michelangelo willingly set to work, and made the most beautiful statue in snow that Florence had ever seen. Piero was delighted and paid him well for the work. It was the only job Piero ever gave him.

Michelangelo returned to his studio and the sleeping Cupid. One day a friend admired the statue and suggested that Michelangelo make it look as if it were very old, for at that time antiques from Greece and Rome were fashionable. Michelangelo was delighted with the idea. He put a coating on the figure which made it look as if it had been in the ground for hundreds of years. The friend took it to Rome and sold it to a cardinal as an antique. Soon the cardinal discovered that he had been fooled, but he was not angry with Michelangelo. He thought the trick was a clever one and invited the young sculptor to visit him in Rome. Michelangelo accepted immediately.

When he arrived in Rome a prosperous banker named Jacopo Gallo asked him to carve a statue. Gallo loved Greek art passionately so Michelangelo chose as his subject the figure of Bacchus, the Greek god of wine. But the figure does not look like the Greek statues of the joyous god. Michelangelo's Bacchus is a handsome youth who stands unsteadily, a cup in his hand and a dazed smile on his face. Perhaps the sculptor was thinking of the youths he had seen in the streets of Rome at night, for the god seems drunk with his own wine.

When the people of Rome saw Michelangelo's masterpiece they were amazed, for the figure was fascinatingly beautiful but startlingly new.

BACCHUS
National Museum, Florence

Photo Anderson

When Gallo saw the statue of Bacchus he decided that Michelangelo was the greatest sculptor in Rome; so he persuaded a well known French cardinal to give a commission to the young Florentine.

"And I, Jacopo Gallo," he wrote in the contract he drew up for Michelangelo and the cardinal, "pledge my word to his Most Reverend Lordship that it shall be the finest work in marble which Rome today can show." Gallo described the subject of the statue. It would be "the Virgin Mary clothed, with the dead Christ in her arms, of the size of a proper man." The subject was a popular one at the time and it was called a "Pieta."

Michelangelo was tired of the pagan gods, and was glad that now at last he was able to tell a story from the Bible. Furiously he began to chip away pieces from the pure white block of marble he had chosen in the quarries of Carrara. He hardly slept at all. Sleep gave him pains in the head and stomach, he wrote to his father, and he ate only a piece of bread when he was hungry.

Ludovico Buonarotti worried about his son in Rome. In his letters he urged Michelangelo to take care of himself. He must keep his head moderately warm, he wrote, have himself rubbed down, but never wash. He recommended for headaches a dish made of herbs and split peas.

Michelangelo paid little attention to his father's advice and worked for a whole year without stopping. Then one day the Pieta was placed in Saint Peter's Church for everyone to see. People were overwhelmed by its beauty. Tenderly the Virgin holds her dead son in her lap, and on her face is an expression of deep sorrow. Some people were surprised that the Mother of Christ had the face of a young girl, but Michelangelo explained that Christ's Mother was eternally young and pure.

Michelangelo was only twenty-five when he finished the Pieta, but he was famous. He knew that he had created a statue of great beauty, so he carved in clear-cut letters the name of MICHELANGELO BUONAROTTI on the broad ribbon which runs across the Virgin's breast.

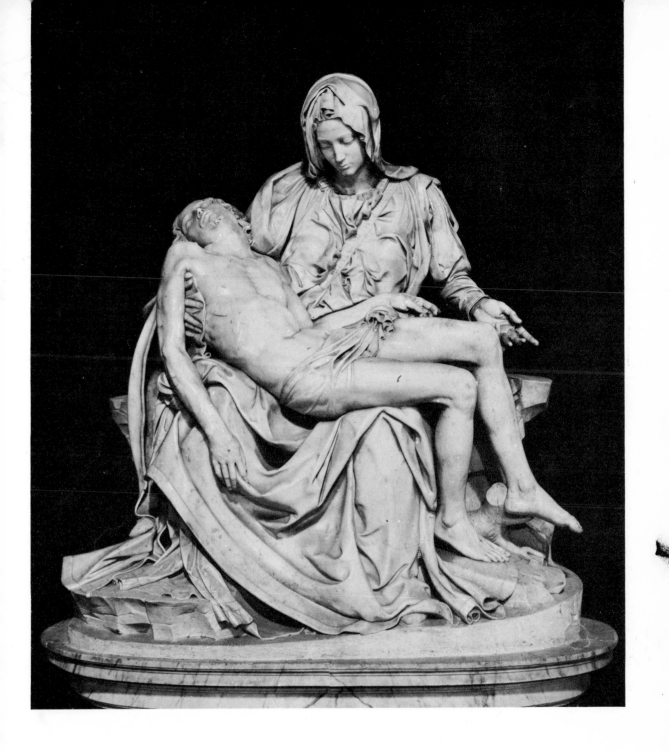

PIETA
Saint Peter's, Rome

Photo Anderson

"Also I remind you," Ludovico Buonarotti wrote to his son in Rome, "that you must make every effort to return as soon as possible, and be assured that when you are here there will be work for you to do."

The Pieta was finished, Michelangelo was famous, and he had made money while he was in Rome. He knew that his family would welcome him now; so, early in the year 1501, Michelangelo returned to Florence.

The city had prospered while he had been away. The streets were filled with richly dressed ladies and gentlemen. Michelangelo, who hated luxuries, looked conspicuous in his dark tunic and cloak and worn boots. But everyone knew that he was the greatest sculptor in Italy. He set himself up in a studio and began to work.

Two prosperous business men from the northern country of Flanders asked him to carve a Madonna and Child for their church in Bruges. When it was finished the merchants shipped it to Flanders and proudly placed it in the church, where it may be seen today.

There is a dreamy look on the face of the stately Madonna. She does not look at the child who leans against her knee. Ten years before Michelangelo had carved the Madonna of the Stairs, and she, too, looks sadly away from the child in her lap. Perhaps Michelangelo thought of his own mother, who had died when he was very little, and expressed in the sad but tender faces of his Madonnas the grief of a mother who must soon leave her son.

MADONNA AND CHILD
Notre Dame, Bruges

In the yard of Florence's City Hall lay a long narrow block of marble. Many years before some sculptor had tried to make it into a statue. The governors of Florence refused to give it away, but when Michelangelo asked to use it the City Council gladly gave it to him.

"Worthy Master Michelangelo," they announced, "has been chosen to fashion . . . that male statue called the Giant."

When the huge block was set on end it was three times as high as Michelangelo. As he studied the tall narrow shape he could almost feel the giant form which lived inside it. He would carve the figure of David, the brave boy who had killed Goliath. He seized his mallet and chisel and went to work.

A shed was built around the block so that no one could see Michelangelo working. Day and night Florentines heard the ring of chisel on stone as the sculptor feverishly chipped away. He worked steadily for two years. Then one day the David was finished. The city governors sent a committee of artists to look at the Giant and decide where it should be placed, but they could not agree on a suitable spot. Finally they decided to ask the opinion of the sculptor himself. Without hesitation Michelangelo said that David should stand at the entrance to one of the palaces in Florence.

With great care David was placed on a cart and pulled slowly through the streets of Florence. People watched, fascinated, as the Giant swayed back and forth in the frame which held it upright. His handsome face stared severely into second story windows as it passed by. For three days Michelangelo anxiously followed David's progress. At night the government appointed a guard to watch over the statue so that no harm should come to it.

On the fourth day a great crowd gathered in front of the palace. The church bells rang out joyously as David was placed on his pedestal. All day the people of Florence celebrated with parades and dancing. The youthful figure of David looked victoriously over the crowd. The Giant had come to life and Michelangelo, like David, had triumphed.

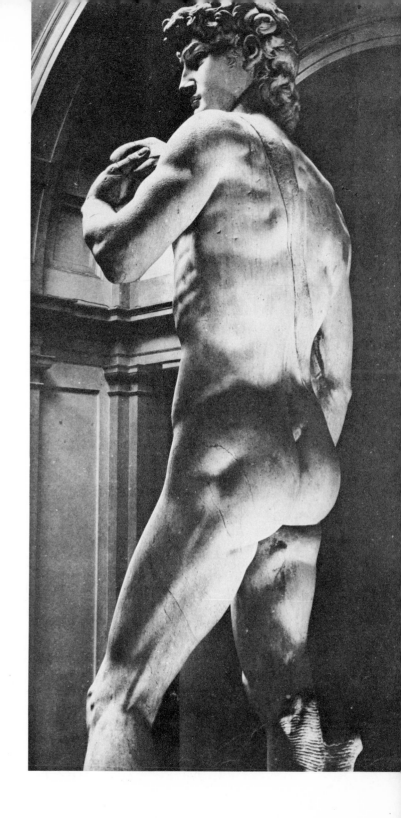

DAVID
Academy of Fine Arts, Florence

Michelangelo was now the most famous sculptor in Italy, but the best known painter was Leonardo da Vinci, who was almost twenty years older. Leonardo was tall and handsome. He had exquisite taste, and a polished manner which irritated the younger artist. While Michelangelo was working on the Giant, Leonardo was decorating one of the walls of Florence's council chamber. Everyone discussed Leonardo's magnificent battle scene, and Michelangelo was jealous.

When the David was finished the City Council asked Michelangelo to decorate a wall of the chamber. The sculptor was elated, for he felt sure he could paint a finer picture than Leonardo's.

He plunged into the work furiously. He, too, chose a battle scene, but it would not look like Leonardo's picture, which was a maze of frenzied horses and screaming warriors. He chose to paint an incident in a battle between the cities of Florence and Pisa, when on one hot summer day the Florentine soldiers had been swimming in a river near Cascina and the Pisan soldiers had attacked them. Michelangelo made a drawing which showed a tangle of nude soldiers hurrying desperately to get into their armor. So beautifully did he draw the figures that they seemed to be carved rather than painted.

Artists from all over Italy came to watch the two painters. Many preferred Leonardo's scene of blood and fury. Others liked Michelangelo's powerful nude figures in violent action.

The contest between the two artists continued furiously. Leonardo had transferred his drawing to the wall and was painting it in glowing oil colors. Michelangelo's drawing was ready for the wall, too, when suddenly he was told to stop. Pope Julius had an important job for him and ordered him to come to Rome immediately. He could not refuse so great an honor. Even the famous Leonardo had never been offered a commission from a Pope. So once again Michelangelo set out for the city of Rome.

Michelangelo's drawing of the Battle of Cascina was never transferred to the council chamber wall, and some years later the sketch disappeared. Today we have only a copy to remind us of the exciting picture which had been discussed so fiercely.

BATTLE OF CASCINA
Holkam Hall, England

Collection of Earl of Leicester

Pope Julius II had great energy and ambition. He wished to be remembered as the most glorious ruler of Christendom, so he ordered Italy's greatest sculptor to design for him a magnificent tomb. Michelangelo drew a picture of a majestic tower of marble. It had eight stories and was decorated with forty gigantic statues.

"When it is finished it will be the most beautiful in the world," he wrote to a friend. Julius was delighted with the design and ordered Michelangelo to hurry to Carrara to choose the marble. The great white blocks were shipped to Rome and piled in the square in front of the cathedral. In a nearby studio Michelangelo started to work.

Julius followed the progress of the tomb excitedly. He had a secret corridor built by which he could visit the sculptor's studio without being seen.

Out of one of the blocks of marble, Michelangelo carved a statue of Moses. The majestic bearded figure is not supposed to be a portrait of Julius, but in the angry gaze of the great leader the sculptor expressed his idea of the fiery and ambitious Pope.

A year went by and Julius began to lose interest in the tomb. The corridor wasn't used any more, and the Pope refused to send Michelangelo any money. Enraged, the sculptor went to see him, but was turned away. Burning with the insult he rushed home and wrote a letter.

"Most Blessed Father," it said, "I have today been driven out of the palace by orders of your Holiness, wherefore I am informing you that if you wish to see me you must look for me elsewhere than in Rome." Then he sold everything in his house, packed up his sketches, and set out on horseback for Florence.

That night five horsemen galloped full speed out of Rome. A few hours later they caught up with Michelangelo and handed him a letter from Julius. "When you have seen this," it said, "return to Rome under penalty of our displeasure."

Angrily Michelangelo shouted at the Pope's messengers that he would never return to Rome, and turning his horse in the direction of Florence he galloped off into the night.

MOSES
TOMB OF JULIUS II
St. Peter's in Vincoli, Rome

Photo Anderson

As soon as Michelangelo arrived in Florence he began once more to work on his battle scene. He paid no attention to the pleading letters from Julius urging him to return to Rome. Six months later, however, the Pope arrived in the nearby city of Bologna and Michelangelo agreed to meet him. He took with him a letter from the governor of Florence. "Michelangelo is an excellent young man," it said. "We cannot recommend him too highly. One has to show him love and treat him kindly and he will perform things that will make the whole world wonder."

When Julius read the letter he decided to pardon his favorite sculptor. He gave Michelangelo his blessing and ordered him to start work on an enormous bronze statue. It was supposed to be the figure of Pope Julius for one of the churches of Bologna. Michelangelo worked on it for a year. When the figure was finished it was placed over the entrance of the church. Julius was delighted and ordered his sculptor to come to Rome immediately. Michelangelo thought of the great blocks of marble piled high in his studio waiting to be carved into statues for the tomb, and decided to obey the Pope's orders.

But Julius had lost interest in his tomb. Anxiously he awaited Michelangelo's arrival in Rome, for he had decided to have the sculptor paint pictures on the ceiling of his private chapel. Michelangelo was downcast when the Pope told him the plan. "Painting is not my trade," he said, but Julius paid no attention. Reluctantly Michelangelo consented to decorate the ceiling.

Michelangelo studied the chapel vaulting high above him. Suddenly there flashed into his mind a terrifying and magnificent plan. He would cover the whole surface with stories from the Bible. The pictures would tell the history of mankind from the creation of the universe to the birth of Christ.

Julius was excited when he saw Michelangelo's sketches and ordered him to start work immediately. One summer day in 1508 Michelangelo climbed the scaffolding of the Sistine Chapel with a roll of sketches under his arm. When he reached the platform under the ceiling he lay on his back and began to paint. For Michelangelo this was the beginning of four long years of torture.

GOD SEPARATING EARTH AND WATER
Sistine Chapel Ceiling, Rome

Photo Anderson

The blazing summer sun beat through the chapel ceiling onto the platform where Michelangelo lay painting. "I am suffering greater hardships than any man endured, ill and with overwhelming labor," he wrote once to his brother in Florence. Paint dropped from his brush into his eyes. His back was arched awkwardly on the hard platform, and his feet hung loosely over the edge. When it grew dark he worked by candle light. He had a mattress brought up to the platform and often he slept there.

"I have no friend of any kind and I do not want any," he wrote, for only in quiet solitude could he bring to life the story of the creation. Occasionally the silence was broken by the sharp ring of a stick on the stone floor. Looking down, Michelangelo could see the white bearded figure of Julius pounding his cane impatiently. Aching in every limb he climbed down the scaffolding. When would the work be finished, Julius wanted to know, and Michelangelo shouted angrily that it would never be finished if the Pope interrupted him all the time. One day in answer to Julius's question the artist snapped back, "When I am able!" Julius was enraged.

"When I am able! When I am able!" he shouted furiously and brought his cane down sharply on Michelangelo's head.

Infuriated, Michelangelo rushed home and started to pack his belongings. But Julius sent a messenger to his house who persuaded him to return to the chapel.

For two years Michelangelo endured the agonies of the scaffolding, but still the ceiling was not finished. Then one day Julius demanded to see the work. In a burst of rage Michelangelo had the scaffolding torn down, and the Pope gazed in wonder at the gigantic paintings high above him. The nine central panels of the vaulted ceiling were filled with magnificent pictures which told the Bible story of the creation, and so beautifully were they painted that the figures seemed to be actually alive.

The side panels of the ceiling were still empty, however, so once more the scaffolding was put up and Michelangelo, ill from over-work, climbed to the platform and started to paint.

CREATION OF MAN
Sistine Chapel Ceiling, Rome

Photo Anderson

Through two more stifling summers and two dark winters Michelangelo lay on his back and painted. He filled some of the side panels of the ceiling with figures of the prophets. Their terrifying warnings must have reminded him of the fiery sermons of the monk, Savonarola, which had made such a deep impression on him when he was young.

Michelangelo read his Bible often and was moved by the thundering words of the prophet Ezekiel, who had said to his people: "So will I send upon you famine and evil beasts and they shall bereave thee: I, the Lord, have spoken it."

All the righteous anger which inspired these words seems to be expressed in the dynamic figure which Michelangelo painted.

PROPHET EZEKIEL
Sistine Chapel Ceiling, Rome

Photo Anderson

A fourth summer passed, fall came, and still Michelangelo lay on his back in the Sistine Chapel. His only companions were the great figures he was bringing to life on the ceiling.

For days he ate only stale bread, which he kept on the platform with him. Often he slept with his boots on, and when he removed them his skin fell off in flakes. He had terrible cramps in his legs and he was almost blind from eyestrain.

In the panels between each prophet he painted magnificent draped figures of the women who were the prophets of ancient Greece. They were called sibyls. One of the loveliest is the Delphic Sibyl, whose beautiful face is full of anguish as if she were predicting a tragic future for mankind.

DELPHIC SIBYL
Sistine Chapel Ceiling, Rome

Photo Anderson

"I have been here a thousand years, I am more exhausted than man ever was," Michelangelo wrote to his father. But his family showed little sympathy for the tortured artist. They continually asked him to send them money. Their letters were full of complaints of every kind.

Exasperated, Michelangelo wrote to his brother in Florence: "I live here in great distress and the utmost physical fatigue. I have no friends and seek none, I have not even time enough to eat what I require; therefor do not put any more burdens upon me, for I could not bear another ounce."

But in spite of the four years of agony, Michelangelo continued to work. Between each prophet and sibyl he painted great pillars. On top of each he placed a magnificent nude figure. The figures do not tell a story. They are not people from the Bible or from the Greek and Roman myths. Michelangelo used them as a kind of ornament because he believed that there was no more beautiful decoration than the human form.

FIGURE
Sistine Chapel Ceiling, Rome

Photo Anderson

"I have finished the chapel which I have been painting. The Pope is very satisfied," Michelangelo wrote to his father in the fall of 1512.

Michelangelo was only thirty-seven, but he felt like a very old man. Four years of agonizing labor had made him almost blind. He had lain so long on his back that when he wanted to read he had to hold his book over his head. But he had finished the chapel at last.

The scaffolding was removed and the people of Rome came to gaze at the ceiling. When they saw Michelangelo's gigantic pictures high above them they gasped in amazement. There were no gorgeous costumes, no bright colors or rich decoration as in the paintings they had seen before. Michelangelo had told his story with three hundred and forty-three magnificent human figures, and so beautifully were they painted that they looked as if they had been carved. Even the best known painters were staggered by the colossal work.

Michelangelo was old and sick. He had toiled alone for four and one half years and had few friends, but he had proved to the world that the great sculptor Michelangelo was also the finest painter alive.

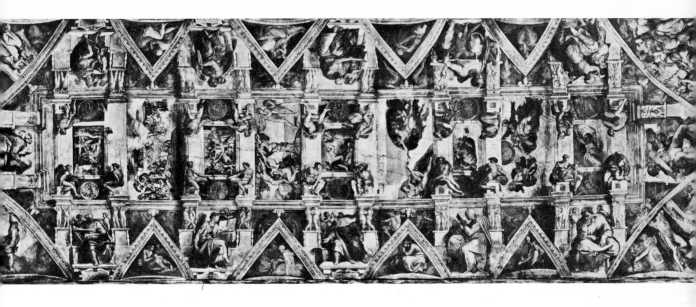

SISTINE CHAPEL CEILING
Rome

Photo Anderson

Pope Julius had only a short time to contemplate the grandeur of the paintings he had waited so long to see. He died four months after the ceiling was completed. He never saw the monumental tomb Michelangelo designed for him, but he ordered in his will that it be completed.

The heirs of Julius drew up a new contract with Michelangelo, which said that the tomb should be smaller. The sculptor made a new drawing which showed only three sides of the monument. The fourth side was placed against the wall. It was only three stories high instead of eight, but it was decorated with twenty-eight marble statues. The contract said the sculptor should not accept any other jobs until the tomb was completed. Michelangelo looked forward to realizing at last his greatest dream.

He returned to the studio where the great blocks of Carrara marble had been lying for over four years. Seizing his mallet and chisel he started furiously to work.

SECOND PROJECT FOR TOMB OF JULIUS II
COPY FROM DRAWING BY MICHELANGELO
BY JACAPO ROCHETTI
Berlin Print Museum

Michelangelo never finished the tomb of Julius II. For forty years he tried to complete the enormous task, but he was interrupted constantly. Finally he agreed to have other artists carry on the work.

Much later, when the sculptor was seventy years old, the tomb was set up in a church in Rome, but it did not look like the imposing eight storied tower he had planned forty years before. The design had been changed so many times that it was far too small for his enormous statues.

At that time Michelangelo lay ill in the home of a rich Roman banker named Roberto Strozzi. When he recovered he gave his host two of the statues he had carved for the tomb. One was the seven foot figure of a slave who struggles to free himself of the bonds which tie him. The captive figure is perhaps an expression of Michelangelo's life, which was a tragic struggle to realize his gigantic dreams.

THE SLAVE
Louvre, Paris

The only statue by Michelangelo which now decorates the tomb of Pope Julius is the angry, bearded figure of Moses that sits majestically at the foot of the monument.

TOMB OF JULIUS II
St. Peter's in Vincoli, Rome

Photo Anderson

After the death of Julius II, Clement VII became Pope. He was a member of the Medici family and had known Michelangelo when he was a boy living in Lorenzo's palace. In memory of his family he decided to build a chapel in the church of San Lorenzo in Florence, and asked Italy's greatest sculptor to design tombs for the Medici rulers. He paid the artist a fine salary and even arranged for him to live in the quiet seclusion of the church while he was doing the work.

Michelangelo labored on the Medici tombs for ten years, but during that time he was harassed by constant interruption. The heirs of Julius demanded that he finish the Pope's tomb. Often he had to abandon his work in the church, and at these times he refused to accept any of Clement's salary.

"I have been ruined by my own conscientiousness," he wrote. "I have only succeeded after a terrible struggle in being poor."

In spite of the many interruptions Michelangelo made two magnificent monuments for the Medici Chapel. One was the tomb of Lorenzo de' Medici, who was a nephew of Michelangelo's good friend, Lorenzo the Magnificent. Lying on top of the tomb are two figures, a man and a woman. The figures are called Dawn and Evening. In a niche above the tomb is seated a handsome man dressed in a Roman uniform, whose face is almost hidden by a splendid helmet.

TOMB OF LORENZO DE' MEDICI
Chapel of San Lorenzo, Florence

Photo Anderson

The statue which sits above the tomb of Lorenzo de' Medici is not a portrait of the duke.

The figure is an expression of Michelangelo's idea of a ruler who is burdened with many problems. His chin is sunk in his hand and he gazes into space as if he were brooding over serious affairs of state.

LORENZO DE' MEDICI
Chapel of San Lorenzo, Florence

Photo Anderson

On a May day in 1527 a crowd of angry Florentines swarmed into the Palace of the Medici shouting *"Popula! Liberta!"* For fifteen years the people of Florence had endured the dictatorship of the Medici and now at last they had revolted. The rulers fled in terror, and Florence became a republic.

But the democratic government did not last long. With the help of Pope Clement the Medici gathered together an army and descended upon the city.

In the seclusion of San Lorenzo, Michelangelo was working on the Medici tombs. Pope Clement continued to pay him a salary, but in his heart Michelangelo had no respect for the Medici dictators. He loved the city of Florence and wanted to help her in her fight for liberty. When the people appointed him governor general in charge of fortifications he was very proud. The great sculptor, painter, and architect now proved that he was also a military engineer. Day and night the short, stocky figure of Michelangelo could be seen standing on the ramparts directing the work.

The siege of Florence lasted for many months. There was so little food that people had to eat cats and dogs. Many died of hunger and sickness. On the eighth of August, 1530, the Florentines opened the gates of the city and the Medici army marched in. The government of the people had ended.

Michelangelo was terror stricken. For days he hid in the ramparts he had designed until the soldiers of Pope Clement discovered him. Reluctantly he consented to return to the church of San Lorenzo and continue the work on the tombs.

He carved a monument for Duke Julien de' Medici, which looks very much like that for Lorenzo. Two figures are lying on the tomb. The man is called Day and the woman, Night.

In a niche above the tomb is a young man dressed in Roman armor. It is not supposed to be Duke Julien, who was weak and sickly. The figure is Michelangelo's idea of a strong ruler. He is a handsome and vigorous young man who sits with his hands resting on a scepter and his head turned as if he were just about to rise and give a command.

TOMB OF JULIEN DE' MEDICI
Chapel of San Lorenzo, Florence

Photo Anderson

One cool September morning the gates of Florence swung open and two men on horseback passed through. Michelangelo and a faithful pupil were on their way to Rome. Michelangelo did not know that he would never see his beloved Florence again. Bravely he had fought for the freedom of his city, and the Medici rulers had taken the freedom away. His home had been taken from him, too, for the brothers and father whom he had loved had died.

The gates of Florence closed slowly behind the riders, and Michelangelo took his last look at the ramparts he had designed for the city he loved so passionately. Four days later he arrived in Rome.

He was now sixty years old and worn out from years of labor. His heart was sad and empty, and in vain he sought the religious faith which he had lost. Three melancholy years he spent in Rome before he met the friend who restored his religion to him.

This friend, Vittoria Colona, was a deeply religious woman, who admired Michelangelo's great genius. Together they went to church, and afterward they would talk for hours about poetry and art. So great was her appreciation of Michelangelo's genius that she inspired him to work. He painted pictures for her and wrote poems to her: "When I am near thee my soul knows no fears," he wrote in one poem.

When Vittoria Colona entered a convent three years later Michelangelo made a drawing of Christ on the cross which he sent to her with a letter. "It has been my earnest wish to perform more for you than for anyone I ever knew upon the world," he wrote.

Then one day Vittoria Colona died. Michelangelo was stupified with grief and loneliness, for he had lost the friend who had given him back his soul. But the deep faith that Vittoria Colona had restored to him stayed with him for the rest of his life.

CHRIST ON THE CROSS
British Museum, London

Michelangelo was studying the end wall of the Sistine Chapel. It was huge, almost square in shape and as high as a five story building. The new Pope, Paul III, had ordered him to cover the wall with one enormous painting of the Last Judgment. The picture would tell the story of the end of the world when Christ came to judge mankind, and it would be the largest picture ever painted.

Michelangelo did not want to paint again. He longed to finish the statues for the tomb of Julius, but he knew it would be dangerous to refuse the orders of the Pope. So one spring day he shut himself in the chapel and started to work.

He was now sixty-three, and he could not work without stopping as he had twenty-five years before. Every two or three days he would throw himself on his bed exhausted. Sometimes he was so weak he could barely hold a brush. One day he lost his balance and fell from the scaffolding. Painfully he pulled himself up from the floor, for he had hurt his leg badly. In agony he limped home and locked the door. He suffered alone for days and would not allow a doctor to see him. Finally a kind friend forced his way into the house and stayed with him until he was well enough to go back to work.

After five and one half years the scaffolding was finally removed. When the people of Rome were allowed to look at the enormous painting, they were stupefied. It was a terrifying whirl of human figures. Michelangelo had painted more than three hundred of them. At the top of the picture is Christ who, with arm upraised, judges from his kingdom in heaven. In the middle are the people who have been judged, and at the bottom are the wicked who have been sent to hell.

Everywhere in Italy people discussed the painting. Many artists said it had miraculous power. Others were shocked by its violence. It was a "mass of wrath, vengeance, and hate" wrote a well known author. But everyone who looked at the Last Judgment was overwhelmed by its terrifying strength.

LAST JUDGMENT
Sistine Chapel, Rome

Photo Anderson

Michelangelo imagined in his painting of the Last Judgment all the terrors of the last days of the world. He pictured the agony of the wicked who were being pulled into hell and the terror and hope of the souls who were being drawn up to heaven. On some of the figures he painted the faces of people he had known. On one figure is the fierce hooked-nose face of Savonarola; another has the face of his friend Vittoria Colona, and the bearded Saint Bartholomew, with flat nose and sad eyes, is supposed to look like Michelangelo himself.

The Last Judgment shocked many people because the figures were not clothed. When Pope Paul sent word that he wanted Michelangelo to cover the figures, the artist replied: "Say to his Holiness that this is a little thing which can be easily put in order; to reform a *painting* is not much trouble."

But Michelangelo did not make any changes in his painting. Several years later a scaffolding was put up in the chapel and another artist painted clothes on Michelangelo's figures. People named the artist "the Breeches Maker."

The picture which now covers the end wall of the Sistine Chapel no longer looks like the one Michelangelo painted. The smoke from candles has blackened it and other artists have changed it, but the titanic genius of the great Michelangelo still lives in the enormous and overpowering painting of the Last Judgment.

SOULS ASCENDING TO HEAVEN:
DETAIL FROM LAST JUDGMENT
Sistine Chapel, Rome

Photo Anderson

A year after the exhausted Michelangelo had finished the Last Judgment he began to decorate the walls of another chapel in Rome. Against his will he had agreed to paint more pictures for Pope Paul, although he had hoped to finish the tomb of Julius.

"You paint with your head and not your hands," he told the Pope. "That is why I can do nothing good so long as I have these preoccupations." But the Pope paid no attention to his protests, so wearily Michelangelo picked up his brushes again and started to work.

It took him eight years to paint two pictures. Every two or three months he would stop work because he felt ill and weak. One day the chapel caught fire, and before the flames could be controlled the roof which protected the paintings had been destroyed. Finally the chapel was repaired and Michelangelo went back to work. He was seventy-five years old when the paintings were finished. Pope Paul did not live to see them.

One picture tells the story of the conversion of Saint Paul and the other the crucifixion of Saint Peter. They are dramatic pictures and very tragic, for Michelangelo suffered greatly while he worked on them. They do not have the energy of the Sistine Chapel paintings, but there is nevertheless great vigor in many of the figures. Michelangelo Buonarotti, although burdened with illness and age, was still an unconquerable painter.

CRUCIFIXION OF SAINT PETER
Pauline Chapel, Rome

Photo Anderson

At the time Michelangelo was working on the chapel paintings he received a letter one day from the Pope telling him that he had been appointed governor and architect of Saint Peter's. Tears of joy sprang to his eyes when he read the news, for Saint Peter's was the church of the Popes in Rome and the most important church in Christendom.

Although Michelangelo was seventy-two years old and he had not finished the chapel paintings or the tomb of Julius, he believed it was his duty to design Saint Peter's Church "as many believe, and I, too," he wrote, "that I have been placed there by God himself." He told the Pope that he would not accept any money for the great task, for only in this way would he truly serve God.

Inspired by religious fervor, he tackled the work with vigor. Jealous artists told the Pope that Michelangelo was not an architect. One assistant started to tear down parts of the church which he had designed. Finally, in desperation, Michelangelo wrote to the Pope. "I intend to ask permission on the first occasion from his Holiness to resign my office." But the Pope would not allow him to stop.

In the blistering heat of summer and in the icy blasts of winter Michelangelo could be seen riding through Rome on his way to Saint Peter's.

"I remain at my post," he wrote, "because I love God and have put my trust in him."

He designed a lofty and magnificent dome to crown the center of the church. The work progressed slowly and Michelangelo's friends feared he would die before the building was finished. Finally they persuaded him to make a wooden model of the dome so that the work could continue after his death.

Michelangelo worked at Saint Peter's for seventeen years, but he did not live to see it completed. Before he died, however, he was able to gaze upon the graceful framework of the noble dome which now crowns Saint Peter's Church in Rome.

CUPOLA OF SAINT PETER'S
Rome

Photo Anderson

"I am weary and ready for death," Michelangelo wrote to a friend when he was eighty-nine years old. "I am burdened, shattered, and torn asunder by endless laboring. There is a wasp buzzing inside me. . . . I am like a scarecrow set up in a freshly sown field. A spider hides in one of my ears and in the other a cricket chirps all night long. . . . I can neither sleep nor snore."

But still Michelangelo continued to toil at Saint Peter's. He would return to his home at night and work on a marble statue which he planned for his own tombstone. By the light of a candle which he placed in his hat, he chipped away huge pieces of stone. Gradually four figures emerged. The center figure of the dead Christ is supported on either side by his mother Mary and Mary Magdalen. Behind is a man in a monk's cowl who leans tenderly over the body of Christ. His bearded face, with its flattened nose and sad eyes, is the face of Michelangelo himself.

One stormy February afternoon the eighty-nine-year-old Michelangelo started to go to Saint Peter's, but when he tried to mount his horse his legs were so weak he could barely move. He stumbled back into his home and sank in a chair by the fire.

Five days later four of his closest friends stood around his bed. In a weak voice he asked one of them to read aloud the story of Christ's death. Then as the four men kneeled down to pray Michelangelo Buonarotti drew his last breath. His great and tortured spirit had found peace at last.

The artist's body did not rest in Rome. Secretly his friends shipped it to Florence. Through streets lined with adoring citizens it was carried to the church of Santa Croce. A great Florentine had come to rest forever in the city he had loved so deeply.

The elaborate monument which now decorates the artist's grave is not the statue he had designed for his own tombstone. It is the work of four sculptors, and is not worthy of the man who created the most magnificent tombs of his age. But the genius of the great Michelangelo will live forever in the glorious works he left behind him.

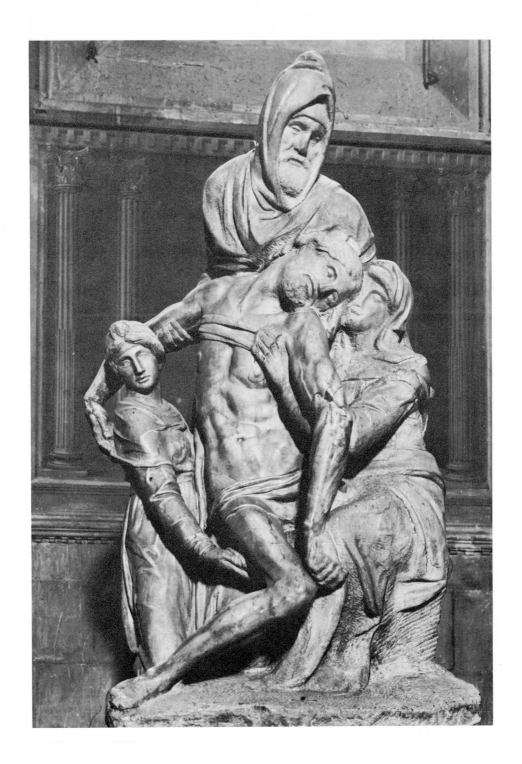

PIETA
Cathedral of Florence

Photo Anderson

ACKNOWLEDGMENTS

I wish to thank Phaidon Press Ltd., London, for giving me permission to reproduce five photographs (Plates opposite pages 12, 18, 26, 28, and 48 in this book) from *The Sculptures of Michelangelo*, by Ludwig Goldscheider, Phaidon Press, 1939, and four photographs (Plates opposite pages 8, 14, 46, and 58 in this book) from *The Drawings of Michelangelo*, by Ludwig Goldscheider, Phaidon Press, 1951.

I also wish to thank the convent of San Domenico in Bologna for the photographs of *The Kneeling Angel with a Candlestick*, reproduced opposite page 20.

BIBLIOGRAPHY

Brion, Marcel: *Michelangelo*. Greystone Press, New York, 1940.

Davies, S. Gerald: *Michelangelo*. M. Methuen & Co., London, 1909.

Demonts, Louis: *Les Dessins de Michelange*. Albert Morancé, Paris, 1921.

Fagan, Louis: *The Art of Michelangelo Buonarotti*. Dulan & Co., London, 1909.

Goldscheider, Ludwig: *The Paintings of Michelangelo*. Phaidon, 1939. *The Sculptures of Michelangelo*. Phaidon, London, 1939. *The Drawings of Michelangelo*. Phaidon, London, 1951.

Gower, Lord Ronald Sutherland: *Great Masters in Painting and Sculpture*. G. Bell & Sons, London, 1903.

Grimm, Herman: *Life of Michelangelo*. Little, Brown, Boston, 1909.

Lerman, Leo: *A Renaissance Profile*. Alfred A. Knopf, New York, 1942.

Papini, Giovanni: *Michelangelo*. E. P. Dutton & Co., New York, 1952.

Rolland, Romain: *La Vie de Michel-ange*. Librarie Hachette, Paris, 1926.

Schevill, Ferdinand: *The Medici*. Harcourt, Brace & Co., New York, 1949.

Symonds, John Addington: *Life of Michelangelo*. Carlton House, New York, 1925.